CULVER'S ROOT

FIELD POPPY

FIVE-SPOT

LESSER CELANDINE

COTONEASTER

CONEFLOWER

SWEET CHERRY TREE

To Ayia and Pappoo—for the garden
you planted that helped start it all

Published by Roaring Brook Press • Roaring Brook Press is a division of Holtzbrinck Publishing Holdings Limited
Partnership • 120 Broadway, New York, NY 10271 • mackids.com • Copyright © 2021 by Lily Williams • All rights reserved.
Library of Congress Control Number: 2020912220 • ISBN 978-1-250-23245-8 • Our books may be purchased in bulk for
promotional, educational, or business use. Please contact your local bookseller or the Macmillan Corporate and Premium
Sales Department at (800) 221-7945 ext. 5442 or by email at MacmillanSpecialMarkets@macmillan.com. • First edition,
2021 • Book design by Mercedes Padró • Printed in China by Toppan Leefung Printing Ltd., Dongguan City, Guangdong
Province • The illustrations in this book were created digitally in Photoshop. • 10 9 8 7 6 5 4

IF BEES
DISAPPEARED

Lily Williams

ROARING BROOK PRESS
NEW YORK

THIS IS KENT, A HISTORIC COUNTY IN THE UNITED KINGDOM.
Kent is known as the "Garden of England" for its rolling hills
and lush landscapes. The creatures that live here are
     fluffy,
        sneaky,
           spiky, and . . .

SMALL.

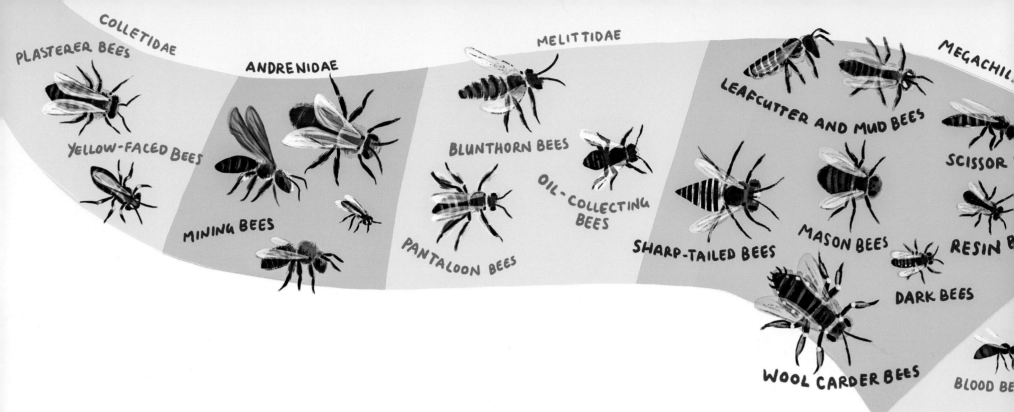

COLLETIDAE
PLASTERER BEES
ANDRENIDAE
MELITTIDAE
MEGACHIL...
LEAFCUTTER AND MUD BEES
YELLOW-FACED BEES
BLUNTHORN BEES
SCISSOR
OIL-COLLECTING BEES
MINING BEES
MASON BEES
RESIN B...
PANTALOON BEES
SHARP-TAILED BEES
DARK BEES
WOOL CARDER BEES
BLOOD BE...

SHORT-FACED B...

Bees are a keystone species, which means they are one of the
most important animals in their ecosystem. Bees' ancestors
first appeared 270 million years ago, and after millions of
years of evolution and a few mass extinctions, honeybees
appeared roughly 35 million years ago in Southeast Asia. Today
there are more than 20,000 species of bees around the globe.

All bees are pollinators, meaning they carry pollen from one plant to another so that the plants can reproduce. Bees are more efficient and successful at pollination than other pollinator sources, like birds and wind.

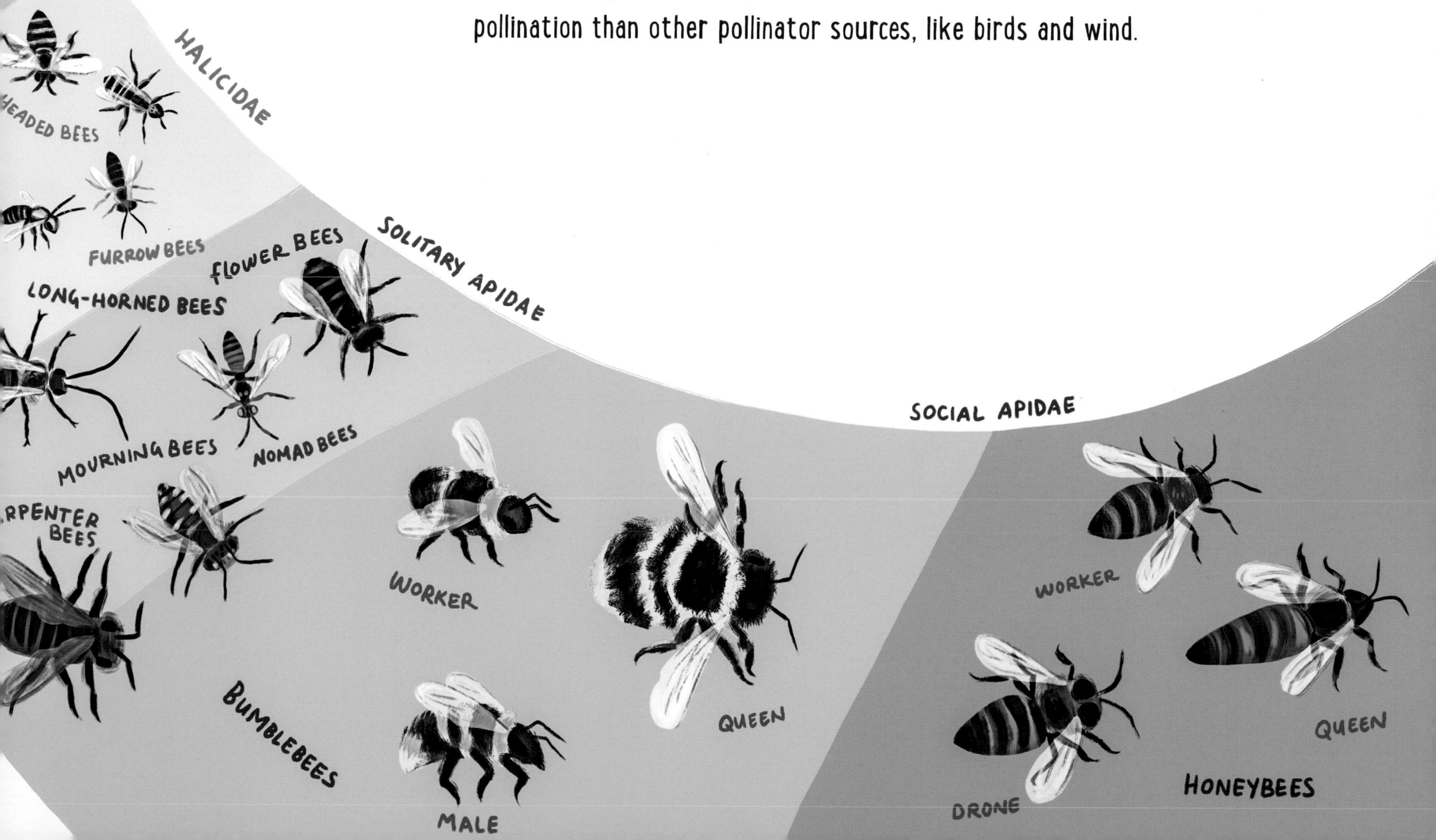

HALICIDAE

HEADED BEES

FURROW BEES

FLOWER BEES

SOLITARY APIDAE

LONG-HORNED BEES

MOURNING BEES

NOMAD BEES

RPENTER BEES

SOCIAL APIDAE

WORKER

QUEEN

WORKER

QUEEN

BUMBLEBEES

MALE

DRONE

HONEYBEES

Honeybees are considered a superorganism. This means all the different parts of the hive act as a single organism and they cannot survive without one another. The queen, who rules the honeybee colony, must remain healthy and mate with the males, called drones, to produce as many baby bees as possible. The rest of the hive is composed of female worker bees. They forage for food, defend their hive, and pollinate flowers.

DRONE

WORKER

QUEEN

Worker honeybees spend their days gathering nectar to feed their colony. During this process, their hairy bodies get covered with pollen, which they then distribute from flower to flower as they slurp up nectar. As the pollen is distributed, the bees are creating a stronger and more diverse flower population.

Unfortunately, today honeybees are threatened by environmental and man-made causes as well as a disease called Colony Collapse Disorder. CCD occurs when a whole colony of bees dies at once. Scientists know that disease, pesticide exposure, lack of foraging habitats, and poor nutrition contribute to CCD; however, the details are not clear as to why this happens. CCD is responsible for most of all hives lost.

If honeybees disappeared . . .

so would most of the plants they pollinate. Wind pollination creates less plant diversity than bee pollination. Plant diversity is important for the strength and health of an environment. While some plants would be able to survive without honeybee pollination, the crops they produce would look different, be less flavorful, and have a shorter life span. The majority of the plants that honeybees pollinate could not survive on wind, bird, or other insect pollination alone.

POLLEN

HONEYBEE POLLINATION

POLLEN

POLLEN

WIND POLLINATION

POLLEN

POLLEN CATCHES ON STIGMAS

If honeybee pollination disappeared . . .

favorite foods like apples, blueberries, avocados, almonds, chocolate, and coffee would become rarer. Fruits are important to many people's diets.

If lots of fruits disappeared . . .

wild fruit-eating birds that rely on these for food, like the European starling, would disappear. This would then affect birds of prey, which rely on smaller birds as a source of food, further disrupting the bird population.

If birds disappeared . . .

there would be no natural pest control in gardens and farms, and the dispersal of seeds from fruit-eating birds would stop. Birds help maintain the health of gardens and farms by consuming hundreds of insects a day. And the seeds fruit-eating birds carry in their gut are dispersed across the land, ensuring biodiversity in fruit plants.

Without bees, birds, and our favorite foods, we would be left with a limited variety of crops.

The loss of these plants, animals, and insects could continue, changing the world as we know it. This unraveling effect, called a trophic cascade, would move from flowers to crops to gardens to cities and to countries, eventually landing . . .

in our own backyards.

From food to medicine to clothing,
bees help keep our lives going.

Thankfully, the news about honeybees is buzzing. With growing urban farm initiatives, bee-responsible growing techniques, and backyard beekeeping, we are able to learn about bees wherever we go.

And maybe we will see that
even the smallest creatures . . .

urban
beekeeping
tours & info

CAN CHANGE THE WORLD.

GLOSSARY

BEEHIVE: the nest or enclosed structure where honeybees live.

BIODIVERSITY: the variety of living organisms in a specific area.

COLONY COLLAPSE DISORDER (CCD): the phenomenon caused when a colony of honeybees disappears, leaving behind their queen. It is unknown what happens to these bees.

KEYSTONE SPECIES: a species that shapes its ecosystem so much that the ecosystem would be far different without that species.

ORGANISM: a life-form (a plant, animal, or single-celled life-form).

PESTICIDE: a substance used to control pests (including plants, insects, or animals). Most pesticides are used to help control crops and can be harmful to the health of plants, insects, and animals.

POLLINATE: to move pollen onto a plant or flower to allow fertilization.

POLLINATOR: an animal or insect that moves pollen from one flower or plant to another, allowing fertilization

SUPERORGANISM: a social unit of organisms unable to survive without one another. Honeybees, ants, coral, and termites are examples of superorganisms.

HONEYBEES ARE IN TROUBLE

All across the world, pollinator populations are in decline. While honeybees are often the face of the pollinator decline, many other pollinators need our help, including wild solitary bees and mason bees. Pesticide usage is believed to be a huge cause of CCD, but Varroa mites are also spreading diseases within bee colonies and to wild bees, and our abundance of farmland worldwide has caused a lack of foraging habitats, leaving bees exposed and vulnerable. Some lost bee population is sustainable, but we are tipping closer to an unsustainable threshold that means other pollinators (birds, wind, and other insects) cannot make up for the loss of bees.

Most of the food we eat relies on honeybee pollination, and so many of the products we use daily, including medicines and clothing, are made possible due to healthy bee pollination and biodiversity in plant life. In order to have diverse food in our markets and pantries, we need to have bee-friendly farming techniques and a more bee-friendly world.

HOW YOU CAN HELP SAVE BEES

If we take small steps now to help bees, we can make a big impact on our future.

• Bee vocal! Tell your friends, tell your parents, tell your community how bees need our help. The more people who know about bees, the more people will care about them and do something to protect them.

• Plant bee-friendly flowers! Bees like simple flowers that they can enter easily, long flowering seasons, and lots of color. Look up what native bee-friendly flowers would be best for where you live.

• Don't overweed your garden or use harsh chemicals. A little bit of untidiness in a garden allows solitary wild bees places to nest and forage.

• Create bee hotels for wild bee species. Wild solitary bees and mason bees may not make honey, but they are great pollinators. Having a healthy wild bee population to supplement honeybees is a great way to help pollination.

• Support local beekeepers by buying their small-batch honey. Responsible and sustainable beekeepers make sure they are leaving enough honey for the bees to be healthy, and by purchasing local honey, you are keeping a beekeeper who is raising healthy local bee populations in business.

• Purchase bee-friendly foods. Some packaging information on foods tells you if the crops were planted in a way that helps bees.

• Get involved with other bee enthusiasts! Scientists appreciate homegrown efforts to aid local bee populations.

• Speak up for the bees! Let your politicians know how you feel about protecting bees and limiting pesticide use. When you are able to, vote with bees in mind!

• Become a beekeeper (with your parents' approval). Beekeeping is an excellent way to keep bee populations strong and to monitor for local disease among bees.

AUTHOR'S NOTE

**The information in this book is a simplified description of a complicated process.
To learn more, start with the bibliography and additional sources listed at the end of this book.**

This book series sprang from my desire to get people to see why sharks are important to our world (*If Sharks Disappeared*). I thought that once people saw how important sharks are and how vulnerable they are to extinction, readers would want to save sharks like I wanted to save sharks. *If Bees Disappeared* is my fourth installment of the If . . . Disappeared series, and with each book, I have gained immense respect for and fallen in love with a new species and the ecosystems they help maintain.

Sometimes, though, I feel there is so much to be done and not enough time. I am overwhelmed by the facts and all the possible ways I can help each of these wonderful creatures. If you ever feel that way, I encourage you to pick one thing and start with that. My hope is that I can inspire you to love these animals the way I do, and then together we can help educate others! The more people know, the more they will be willing to take steps to protect our planet. If bees have taught us anything, it's that small efforts add up and make a big impact.

ACKNOWLEDGMENTS

This book would not exist without the following people who aided and encouraged me in my research and exploration: my family—who always let me fly; Minju Chang of BookStop Literary Agency, who helped me earn my stripes; Emily Feinberg of Roaring Brook Press, who is the bee's knees; the art direction team that has made these books soar over the years; the publicity and school and library teams that create buzz; Anna Lee, who introduced me to her hive and is a queen; and *you*, for listening, reading, and helping spread the word about pollinators. Let's save the bees!

BIBLIOGRAPHY

Benjamin, Alison. "Why Bees Are the Most Invaluable Species." *Guardian* (US edition). November 21, 2008. theguardian.
com/environment/blog/2008/nov/21/wildlife-endangeredspecies.

Chadwick, Fergus, et al. *The Bee Book*. New York: DK, 2016.

Cirino, Erica. "What Do the Birds and the Bees Have to Do with Global Food Supply?" *Audubon*. March 10, 2016. audubon.
org/news/what-do-birds-and-bees-have-do-global-food-supply.

Cornell Lab of Ornithology. "European Starling Overview." *All About Birds*. Accessed 2019. allaboutbirds.org/guide/
European_Starling/overview.

Harwood, Jessica, et al. "Bird Ecology." CK-12 Foundation. Last modified July 3, 2019. ck12.org/biology/bird-ecology/lesson/
Importance-of-Birds-MS-LS/.

Kent Bee-Keepers' Association. "Welcome to the Kent Bee-Keepers' Association (KBKA) Website." Accessed 2019. kbka.org.uk/.

"Kent, Garden of England." Travel About Britain. Accessed 2019. travelaboutbritain.com/information/garden-of-england.php.

Kent Wildlife Trust. "Wildlife Species Explorer—Mammals." Accessed 2019. kentwildlifetrust.org.uk/wildlife-explorer/mammals.

Lee, Anna. "Bees and Beekeeping." Personal interview, 2019.

Mayntz, Melissa. "Birds That Eat Fruit—Including Apples!" *The Spruce*, Dotdash. October 16, 2019. thespruce.com/birds-
that-eat-fruit-including-apples-385829.

O'Toole, Christopher. *Bees: A Natural History*. Buffalo, NY: Firefly Books, 2013.

Palmer, Brian. "Would a World Without Bees Be a World Without Us?" NRDC. May 18, 2015. nrdc.org/onearth/would-
world-without-bees-be-world-without-us.

SciShow. "Are the Bees Okay Now?" YouTube. January 5, 2019. youtube.com/watch?v=GjyzYQWU2sg.

Uppsala Universitet. "Evolutionary History of Honeybees Revealed by Genomics." *ScienceDaily*. August 24, 2014.
sciencedaily.com/releases/2014/08/140824152245.htm.

Zuckerman, Catherine. "What Happens If the Honeybees Disappear?" *National Geographic*. October 3, 2017.
nationalgeographic.com/magazine/2017/10/explore-animals-bees/.

ADDITIONAL SOURCES

The Bee Book, published by DK and written by Fergus Chadwick, Steve Alton, Emma Sarah Tennant,
Bill Fitzmaurice, and Judy Earl

QueenSpotting: Meet the Remarkable Queen Bee and Discover the Drama at the Heart of the Hive, published by Storey
Publishing and written by Hilary Kearney

OREGANO

ROSEMARY

SEA HOLLY

PEONY

APPLE TREE

HEATHER

PINCUSHION FLOWER